THE
MARCH
BABY

By Noel Streatfeild and available from Headline

The January Baby

The February Baby

The March Baby

The April Baby

The May Baby

The June Baby

The July Baby

The August Baby

The September Baby

The October Baby

The November Baby

The December Baby

THE
March
BABY

★

Noel Streatfeild

Copyright © Noel Streatfeild 1959
Copyright © The beneficiaries of the estate of Noel Streatfeild 1986
Excluding the illustrations on pages iii, v, 7, 26, 30, 31, 50, 65,
68, 78, 83 © Becky Cameron 2023

The right of Noel Streatfeild to be identified as the Author of the Work has been
asserted by her in accordance with the Copyright, Designs and Patents Act 1988.

First published in 1959
This edition published in 2023 by Headline Home
an imprint of Headline Publishing Group

I

Apart from any use permitted under UK copyright law, this publication may
only be reproduced, stored, or transmitted, in any form, or by any means, with prior
permission in writing of the publishers or, in the case of reprographic production,
in accordance with the terms of licences issued by the Copyright Licensing Agency.

Every effort has been made to fulfil requirements with regard to reproducing copyright material.
The author and publisher will be glad to rectify any omissions at the earliest opportunity.

Cataloguing in Publication Data is available from the British Library

Hardback ISBN 978 1 0354 0843 6
eISBN 978 1 0354 0844 3

Typeset in 14.75/15pt Centaur MT Pro by Jouve (UK), Milton Keynes

Printed and bound in Great Britain by Clays Ltd, Elcograf S.p.A.

MIX
Paper | Supporting
responsible forestry
FSC® C104740
www.fsc.org

Headline's policy is to use papers that are natural, renewable and recyclable
products and made from wood grown in well-managed forests and other
controlled sources. The logging and manufacturing processes are expected
to conform to the environmental regulations of the country of origin.

HEADLINE PUBLISHING GROUP
An Hachette UK Company
Carmelite House
50 Victoria Embankment
London EC4Y 0DZ

www.headline.co.uk
www.hachette.co.uk

CONTENTS

This book contains examples of historical cures and home remedies. These are included for historical interest only and should not be followed. If your child is unwell, consult a doctor or other medical professional. Neither the author nor the publisher accept any liability for any loss or damage caused by the application of any of the information or suggestions in this book.

THE little March hare has arrived. Telephones have buzzed, the great news has flown from mouth to mouth. All the questions have been answered. The weight at birth, the colour of the eyes, and hair, and how the mother is doing. Now the relations and friends are relaxed, for they have had the longed for message, 'Mother and baby are doing well.'

1

March is daffodil month. Ever since the good news got around flowers, with daffodils predominating, have been arriving. So many perhaps that however sweet the smile given to you, the mother, you are conscious that out of ear-shot someone is saying, 'More flowers! What on earth am I going to put these in?'

Spring is in the air. Every shop window has its reminders. Small skipping blacknosed lambs, pussy palm with little artificial birds on the sprigs, chestnut branches for sale, with sticky buds showing faintly green at the tips.

Family and friends have gazed and wondered. It would be nice to bring a spring-like offering to mother and baby, but will a black-nosed lamb, birds or pussy willow, or chestnut buds really be a riot at the bedside?

Fruit is a nice present but March is such a dull month for fruit. It may be possible to find a ripe avocado, but more likely every shop admits theirs are as hard as rocks, and won't be fit to eat for another week. There are

3

some South African plums which can be delicious, but also can be curiously flavourless. This leaves the old faithfuls oranges, apples, bananas, and grapes, and somehow these seem a dull present, everybody is a mite tired of oranges, apples, bananas, and grapes; if only strawberries were ripe!

Something to wear is a lovely present, but March is not an easy month for giving bed-jackets. Spring may be in the air, but the winds of March can be perishing cold. It would be lovely to present one of those diaphanous little negligées which look so enchanting in the shops, but would it be put away in a drawer with many 'tuts,' as soon as the back is turned, and the new mother buttoned firmly back into something quilted or woolly? It is humiliating

to feel a gift which probably has cost ill-afforded money was really rather a silly one.

Few friends and relations have had the self-control to keep the baby clothes they have bought or made until the baby has actually

arrived. For one good reason: if a blue baby coat has been knitted nothing can be done if it should have been pink for a little girl. Before the arrival, coats of any colour are received rapturously, but afterwards mistakes in the colour schemes have to be apologised for. So the chances are it is not baby clothes we bring in our parcels.

Years of wondering what present would she like, have resulted in this book. Obviously mothers of new babies do not want to think of much else but the newcomer. Here then is nothing but information about March babies. Famous babies, born in March, writings about and by March babies, and the signs and portents attached to March babies. As well, though probably few will need it, a list of names suitable for March babies. Obviously most parents have known for the last nine months what they will call their baby, whether it is a boy or a girl, in fact usually it has had a name, not always a polite one, since it was first expected, but there are always exceptions, the mother who cannot make up her mind, or the father who insists on a family name with which nothing seems to go. For such the list of names and their meanings may prove helpful.

For the zodiac signs there should, of course, be marked differences between Pisces and Aries babies. The list of the famous March babies may, however, raise doubts in the mind. Would it not seem likely that Saint Catherine of Sienna was full of sympathy and gave herself entirely for others? Yet she was born

not under Pisces, but on the 25th under Aries, and should have shown a progressive and aggressive spirit. Did Madame Malibran and Mahomet II really have the qualities we recognise today in Tommy Trinder, General Norstad and Malcolm Muggeridge? An interesting thought on which the mother of a March baby might brood.

NAMES
for the
MARCH
BABY

THE Romans made March the first month of the year in their calendar, and dedicated it to Mars, the god of war, so whether we like it or not, March names have war-like meanings. There are several to choose from, and all mean 'of Mars', amongst them are *Marcella, Marcia, Marina,* and *Martine,* and for boys *Mark, Martin, Marcus,* and *Marcellus.*

The theme of war and objects connected with it blows like a March gale through the list, the most unlikely being *Averil* which means 'wild boar battle-maid'. *Avice* means 'war-refuge', *Berenice* 'bringer of victory', *Brenda* 'sword-blade', *Clotilda* 'famous battle-maid', *Eda* and *Edith* mean 'prosperous war'. *Lois* and *Eloise* 'famous war', *Eunice* 'fortunate victory', and *Victoria* 'victory'. Battle spears provide meanings for several names: *Geraldine* means

'spear-wielder', *Gertrude* and *Truda* 'spear strength', *Hilda* and *Hildegard* 'battle-wand'. *Matilda* and *Maud* 'mighty battle-maid', and to crown the picture *Whilhelmina* which means 'stout helmet'.

Here are a group of names for boys to do with war. *Alastair, Alec, Alex, Alexander, Alick*

and *Saunder* all mean 'defending men'. *Alexis* and *Hector* mean 'defender'. *Aloysius*, *Lewis*, *Lodowick* and *Louis* mean 'famous war'. *Alphonso* means 'nobly eager for battle', *Anselm* 'divine helmet', *Barry* 'spear', *Boris* 'fight', *Brand* and *Brendan* 'sword-blade', *Cedric* 'war chief', *Duncan* 'brown warrior', *Edgar* 'felicitious spear', *Egbert* 'sword-bright', *Egmond* and *Egmont* 'sword protection', *Gerald* 'spear wielder', *Gerard* 'firm spear', *Gervais*, *Gervaise*, *Gervase*, *Jarvis* and *Jervis* all mean 'spear-eagerness' which judging by the variations was a much sought-after quality at one time. *Harold* means 'army power',

Harvey 'warrior-war', *Herbert* 'bright army,' and *Hereward* 'army protection'.

Herman which recalls unhappy memories really means 'army man', *Hildebrand* 'battle-sword', *Kenelm* 'bold helmet', *Lachlan* 'war-like', *Luther* 'famous warrior', *Oscar* 'divine spear', *Roger* 'spear of fame', *Stanislaus* 'camp glory', *William* 'resolute helmet', and nobody needs to be told the meaning of *Victor*, and a similar name is *Vincent* which means 'conquering'.

March is rich in the number of days which commemorate saints. Here in their date order is a list of them and the names associated with them.

The 1st of March is St David's Day, the patron saint of Wales. The name *David* means 'friend', and for a girl there is *Cara* which means 'a rich friend', and *Edwina* which means 'friendly'. Many

other Welsh names are lovely, so they are added to the list: *Blodwen* which means 'white flower', *Bronwen* 'white breast', *Dilys* 'genuine', *Gwenda* 'white', and *Olwen* 'white track'.

The 12th of March is St Gregory's Day. *Gregory* means 'to be watchful'.

The 17th is St Patrick's Day, the patron saint of Ireland. *Patrick* means 'patrician'. On St Patrick's Day Irish names are suitable: *Aidan* which means 'fire', as do *Aine*, *Aithne*, and *Eithne*. Also from Ireland comes *Deidre* or *Derdre* which mean 'the raging one'.

The 18th March is the day of St Edward. *Edward* means 'rich ward'. The 19th is

St Joseph's Day. *Joseph* means 'may Jehovah increase', as does *Josephine*, of which *Josette* is a variation.

The day of St Benedict, which means 'blessed', is 21st March, officially the first day of spring when the days and the nights are each twelve hours long. *Benedicta, Benita* and *Gwyneth* all mean 'blessed' too.

The 25th of March is Lady Day. *Martha, Martita* and *Marta* all mean 'lady'.

March is the month for sowing, so what about *Georgia, Georgiana* or *Georgina*, all of which mean 'tiller of the soil', or *Hortensia* which means 'gardener'?

March was used as a boy's name long ago, but it did not mean 'hare', as might be supposed, but it came from a word for 'horse'.

GIFTS
for the
MARCH
BABY

19

IF any godparent would like to give a
piece of jewellery to the March baby, the
right stone is the aquamarine, and
mothers of March babies will envy their child,
for the clear sea-blue stone is not only
attractive to wear, but has wonderful qualities
associated with it. What could be more
satisfactory to wear than an emblem which
means happiness and everlasting youth?

'It renders the Bearer of it chearful;
preserves and increases Conjugal Love; being
hung to the Neck, it drives away idle Dreams;
it cures the Distempers of the Throat and
Jaws, and all Disorders proceding from the
Humidity of the Head, and is a Preservative
against them; being taken mixed with an equal

Quantity of Silver, it cures the Leprosy. The Water in which it has been put, is good for the Eyes; and if drank, it dispels Heaviness, and cures the Indispositions of the Liver. It helps pregnant Women in preventing abortive Births, and other Incommodities to which they are liable.'

Leonardus, *The Mirror of Stones,* 1750.

The old custom of arranging flowers so that they bring a message should be revived for a March baby. So if your child should receive a nosegay of crown imperials and a bunch of violets, the meaning is power and modesty. Modesty of course belongs to the violet, and power to the crown imperial.

If your baby was born between the 1st and the 20th of March read pages 26 and 27, but if between the 21st and the 31st of March, skip to pages 28 and 29.

22

UNDER
WHAT STARS WAS
MY BABY
BORN?

PISCES
The Fishes
20th February–20th March

ARIES
The Ram
21st March–20th April

TAURUS
The Bull
21st April–21st May

GEMINI
The Twins
22nd May–21st June

CANCER
The Crab
22nd June–23rd July

LEO
The Lion
24th July–23rd August

24

VIRGO
The Virgin

24th August–23rd September

LIBRA
The Scales

24th September–23rd October

SCORPIO
The Scorpion

24th October–22nd November

SAGITTARIUS
The Archer

23rd November–21st December

CAPRICORN
The Sea Goat

22nd December–20th January

AQUARIUS
The Water Bearer

21st January–19th February

Pisces, the Fishes
20th February—20th March

PEOPLE born under Pisces are full of sympathy and apt to give themselves up entirely for others. Sensitive and anxious, they are as vulnerable as they are affectionate and loving. Though not lacking in self-esteem, they need to cultivate self-reliance. Unassuming in manner and not at their best in conversation, they are not easily understood and appreciated. They are restless, yet creatures of habit. Their very duality makes the special virtue of Pisces people their capacity to achieve peace.

For the Pisces Baby

Lucky to wear an amethyst.
Lucky stones are granite, sandstone.
Lucky metal is tin.
The Pisces baby's colour is violet.
Lucky number is 3.
Luckiest day of the week is Thursday.

Aries, the Ram
21st March–20th April

ARIES, the most positive sign of the zodiac, gives a very progressive and aggressive spirit. Aries people are full of energy, hot and impulsive in their passions, large in their perceptions. Themselves basically ungovernable, they are ambitious to lead others and are more often than not well capable of doing so. They are generous, but not to the sacrifice of their own ends. People born under Aries may tend to be changeable and irritable, but where courage is needed they are, above all others, dauntless.

For the Aries Baby

Lucky to wear a ruby.
Lucky stone is flint.
Lucky metal is iron.
The Aries baby's colour is red.
Lucky number is 9.
Luckiest day of the week is Tuesday.

BABIES BORN
ON
THE SAME DAY
AS
YOUR BABY

SHOULD you feel pleased that your baby was born on a particular day? Is there any truth in what the astrologers say about some birth days having special advantages, that babies born under Pisces are like this, whereas babies born under Aries are like that? Have a look at the well-known people in this list before you make up your mind.

1st   Marcel Prévost, 1862. Giles Lytton Strachey, 1880. David Niven, 1910.

2nd   Juvenal, c. 40. Robert II of Scotland, 1316. Pope Leo XIII, 1810. Smetana, 1824. Pope Pius XII, 1876. Jennifer Jones, 1920.

3rd   William Godwin, 1756. Macready, 1793. Alexander Graham Bell, 1847. Sir Henry Wood, 1870. Ada Reeve, 1874.

General Alfred Gruenther, 1899. Ronald Searle, 1920.

4th   Don Pedro of Portugal, 1394. Sir Henry Raeburn, 1756. Joan Greenwood, 1921.

5th   David II of Scotland, 1324. Gerardus Mercator, 1512. Rosa Luxemburg, 1870. Lord Beveridge, 1879. Rex Harrison, 1908. David Astor, 1912.

6th   Michelangelo, 1475. Stringer Lawrence, 1697. Cardinal York, 1725. Sir Charles Napier, 1786. Elizabeth Barrett Browning, 1806.

7th   Sir Edwin Landseer, 1802. T. G. Masaryk, 1850. Maurice Ravel, 1875. Anna Magnani, 1908.

8th   Saint John of God, 1495. Austen Layard, 1817. Ruggiero Leoncavallo, 1858. Kenneth Grahame, 1859.

9th   Amerigo Vespucci, 1451. St Aloysius, 1568. William Cobbett, 1762. Dr Joseph Franz Gall, 1775. Ernest Bevin, 1881. Molotov, 1890. V. Sackville-West, 1892.

10th   Ferdinand V of Castile, 1452. Marcellus Malpighi, 1628. Admiral John Benbow,

1653. Louisa Henrietta of Orange, 1776. Raven Hill, 1867. Tamara Karsavina, 1885. Arthur Honegger, 1892.

11th   Torquato Tasso, 1544. Hubert Scott-Paine, 1891. Frederick IX of Denmark, 1899. Harold Wilson, 1916.

12th   Bishop George Berkeley, 1685. Lady Hester Stanhope, 1776. John Lawrence Toole, 1832. Kemal Atatürk, 1881.

13th   Pope Innocent XII, 1615. Dr Joseph Priestley, 1733. Joseph II of the Holy Roman Empire, 1741. Charles, Earl Grey, 1764. Sir Hugh Walpole, 1884. Juan Gris, 1887.

14th   Johann Strauss, 1804. Paul Ehrlich, 1854. Albert Einstein, 1879. John McCallum, 1918.

15th   Dame Madge Kendal, 1848. Lord Catto, 1879. Lord Salter, 1881. Lord Layton, 1884. Viscount Chandos of Aldershot, 1893. John Gregson, 1919.

16th   Caroline Herschel, 1750. Lady Anne Hamilton, 1766. Georg Simon Ohm, 1787. Jean Forbes-Robertson, 1905. Norman Wooland, 1910.

17th   James IV of Scotland, 1473. Captain
        Oates, 1880. Patricia Hornsby-Smith,
        1914.
18th   Stéphane Mallarmé, 1842. Rimsky-
        Korsakov, 1844. Rudolf Diesel, 1858.
        Neville Chamberlain, 1869. Robert
        Donat, 1905.
19th   David Livingstone, 1813. Alfred von
        Tirpitz, 1849. Wilkie Bard, 1874. Sarah
        Gertrude Millin, 1889. Frederic Joliot-
        Curie, 1900.
20th   Malcolm IV of Scotland, 1142. Cecily
        of York, 1469. Ibsen, 1828. René
        Coty, 1882. Gigli, 1890. Michael Redgrave,
        1908. Hugh McDermott, 1912.
21st   Robert Bruce, King of Scotland, 1274.
        Bach, 1685. Jean Paul, 1763. Benito
        Juárez, 1806. Gogol, 1809. Albert
        Chevalier, 1861.
22nd   William I of Germany, 1797. Rosa
        Bonheur, 1822. Carl Rosa, 1842. Robert
        Millikan, 1868. Nicholas Montsarrat,
        1910.
23rd   Margaret of Anjou, 1430. Laplace, 1749.
        Sir Charles Wyndham, 1837. Frank

Sargeson, 1903. Joan Crawford, 1908. Dr Roger Bannister, 1929.

24th   Mahomet II, 1430. Madame Malibran, 1808. Malcolm Muggeridge, 1903. General Lauris Norstad, 1907. Tommy Trinder, 1909.

25th   Henry II, 1133. Saint Catherine of Siena, 1347. Arturo Toscanini, 1867. Béla Bartok, 1881. Haydn Wood, 1882.

26th   Gesner, 1516. A. E. Housman, 1859. Sir Gerald du Maurier, 1873. Tennessee Williams, 1912.

27th   Comte de Vigny, 1797. Roentgen, 1845. A. P. Elkin, 1891. Semprini, 1908.

28th   Raphael, 1483. Mussorgsky, 1835. Aristide Briand, 1862. Gorki, 1868. Beria, 1899. Flora Robson, 1902. Dirk Bogarde, 1921.

29th   Joseph Guillotin, 1783. Sir Edward Geoffrey Stanley, 14th Earl of Derby, 1799. Sir Edwin Lutyens, 1869. Sir William Walton, 1902. Geoffrey Duke, 1923.

30th   Maimonides, 1135. Goya, 1746. Anna Sewell, 1820. Verlaine, 1844. Van Gogh, 1853.

31st   Pope Pius IV, 1499. Descartes, 1596.
Andrew Marvell, 1621. Haydn, 1732.
Edward Fitzgerald, 1809. Andrew
Lang, 1844. Duke of Gloucester, 1900.

THE
UPBRINGING
OF MARCH
BABIES
OF
THE
PAST

FROM a letter written by Mrs Delany to her sister, dated 1st March, 1744:

'I am very much concerned for my dear godson, but hope before this reaches you that his ague will have left him. Two *infallible receipts* I must insert before I proceed further.

First. Pounded ginger, made into a paste with brandy, spread on sheep's leather, and a plaister of it laid over the navel.

Secondly. A spider put into a goose-quill, well sealed and secured, and hung about the child's neck as low as the pit of his stomach. Either of these I am assured will ease. *Probatum est.*'

Then, on 6th March:

'I hope before this arrives he will have lost every symptom of complaint, if not, it is best to give him bark in the only way children can take it, which very seldom fails. I have sent a prescription from Mrs Montague and Mr Clark. Everybody agrees you should give the child meat now; he may eat meat three times a week, and pudding or panada the other days. Sometimes sheep's trotters, which are both innocent and nourishing; and make him to be jumbled about a good deal for fear of falling into the rickets, and throw away his wormwood draughts, for they *signify nothing* for an ague. Have an attention to him about worms, which are the cause of most children's illness.'

The Autobiography and Correspondence of Mrs Delany, 1861.

CLOTHING

The manner of dressing infants three centuries ago was enough to cripple them, without any other malpractices in their nurseries. The unfortunate little creatures, as soon as they were born, were swathed, or swaddled, in a number of rollers; their arms were bound down to their sides, and their legs straight and close together, after the exact pattern of an Egyptian mummy. This operation was called swaddling, and when completed, the miserable babe looked precisely like a chrysalis, with a little round face at the top, clad in a cap or hood, without a border.

Strickland, *Lives of the Queens of England*, 1875.

In 1788 William Godwin took as a pupil, gratuitously, his kinsman, Thomas Cooper, then twelve years of age, who had just lost his father in the East Indies. Daily . . . and indeed hourly . . . squabbling lasted so long as Tom Cooper continued with Godwin, till Cooper was nearly seventeen; and he from time to time relieved his feelings and refreshed his

memory by writing down his tutor's 'pointed and humiliating words.' Here is one such memorandum:

In my presence
He called me *a foolish wretch.*
He said *I had a wicked heart.*
He would *thrash me.*
(Does he think I would submit quietly?)

In my absence
I am called *a Brute.*
I am compared to *a Viper.*

He went out *merely to avoid me.*
I am *a Tiger.*
I have *a black heart.*
No justice in it.
No proper feelings.

He has no enmity to my *person*, yet he hates me. I suppose he means by that that he does not think me very ugly, etc., etc.

This paper he, in a pet, addressed to Mr Godwin, and by design or accident put it in his way. Godwin's letter in reply begins thus:

April 19, 1790.

My dear Boy ... I am more pleased than displeased with the paper I have just seen. It discovers a degree of sensibility that may be of the greatest use to you, though I will endeavour to convince you that it is wrongly applied ...

William Godwin, 1876.

EDUCATION

When we examine the merciless school drill frequently enforced, the wonder is, not that it does extreme injury, but that it can be borne at all. Take the instance given by Sir John Forbes, from personal knowledge; and which he asserts, after much inquiry, to be an average sample of the middle-class girls'-school system throughout England.

Omitting detailed divisions of time, we quote the summary of the twenty-four hours.

In bed . . . . 9 hrs.
    (the younger, 10 hrs.)
In school, at their studies and
  tasks . . . . 9 hrs.
In school, or in the house, the
  elder at optional studies or

work, the younger at play .	3 ½ hrs.
(the younger, 2 ½ hrs.)	
At meals	1 ½ hrs.
Exercise in the open air, in the shape of a formal walk, often with lesson-books in hand, and even this only when the weather is fine at the appointed time .	1 hrs.
	24 hrs.

And what are the results of this 'astounding regimen,' as Sir John Forbes terms it? Of course feebleness, pallor, want of spirits, general ill-health. But he describes something more. This utter disregard of physical welfare, out of extreme anxiety to cultivate the mind . . . this prolonged exercise of brain and deficient exercise of limbs . . . he found to be habitually followed, not only by disordered functions but by malformation. He says: 'We lately visited, in a large town, a boarding-school containing forty girls; and we learnt, on close and accurate inquiry, that there was *not one* of the girls who had been at the school two years (and the majority

46

had been as long) that was not more or less *crooked!*'

It may be that since 1833, when this was written, some improvement has taken place. We hope it has.

Herbert Spencer, *Education*, 1861.

'No child under the Age of Eight Years shall be employed in any Agricultural Gang.'

Law passed in 1867.

LENT-CROCKING

Parties of young people, during Lent, go to the most noted farmhouses, and sing, in order to obtain a *crock* or cake, an old song beginning:

> I see by the latch
> There is something to catch;
> I see by the string
> The good dame's within;
> Give a cake, for I've none;
> At the door goes a stone.
> Come give, and I'm gone.

'If invited in,' says Mrs Bray, 'a cake, a cup of cider, and a health followed. If not invited in, the sport consisted in battering the house door with stones, because not open to hospitality. Then the assailant would run away, be followed and caught, and brought back again as prisoner, and had to undergo the punishment of roasting the shoe. This consisted in an old shoe being hung up before the fire, which the culprit was obliged to keep in a constant whirl, roasting himself as well as the shoe, till some damsel took compassion on him, and let him go; in this case he was to treat her with a little present at the next fair.'

Halliwell, *Popular Rhymes and Nursery Tales*, 1849.

Mid-Lent Sunday. On this day at Seville there is an usage evidently the remains of an old custom. Children of all ranks, poor and gentle, appear in the streets fantastically dressed, somewhat like English chimney-sweepers on May-day, with caps of gilt and coloured paper, and coats made of the crusade bulls of the preceding year. During the whole day they make an incessant din with drums and rattles, and cry, 'Saw down the old woman.' At midnight, parties of the commonalty parade the streets, knock at every door, repeat the same cries, and conclude by sawing in two the figure of an old woman representing Lent. This division is emblematical of Mid-Lent.

Hone, *Every-Day Book*, 1838.

DISTINGUISHED
MARCH
BABIES

AUGUSTUS J. C. HARE
born March 1834.

I remember one very hot summer's day in 1839, when I had been very naughty over my lessons ... that Uncle Julius was summoned. He arrived, and I was sent upstairs to 'prepare.' Then, as I knew I was going to be whipped anyway, I thought I might as well do something horrible to be whipped *for*, and, as soon as I reached the head of the stairs, gave three of the most awful, appalling and eldrich shrieks that ever were heard in Hurstmonceaux. Then I fled for my life. Through the nursery was a small bedroom, in which Lea slept, and here I knew that a large black travelling "imperial" was kept under the bed. Under the bed I crawled, and wedged myself into the narrow space behind the imperial, between it and the wall. I was only just in time. In an instant all the household ... mother, uncle, servants ... were in motion, and a search was on foot all over the house. I turn cold still when I remember the agony of fright with which I heard Uncle Julius enter the nursery, and then, with which, through a chink, I could see his large feet moving about the very room in which I was. He *looked under the bed*, but he saw only a large black box. I held my breath, motionless, and he turned away. Others looked under the bed too; but my concealment was effectual.

I lay under the bed for an hour ... stifling ... agonised. Then all sounds died away, and I knew that the search in the house was over, and that they were searching the garden. At last my curiosity would no longer allow me to be still, and I crept from under the bed and crawled to the window of my mother's bedroom, whence I could overlook the garden without being seen. Every dark shrub, every odd corner was being ransacked. The whole household and the gardeners were engaged in the pursuit. At last I could see by their actions . . . for I could not hear words . . . that a dreadful idea had presented itself. In my paroxysms I had rushed down the steep bank, and tumbled or thrown myself into the pond! I saw my mother look very wretched and Uncle Julius try to calm her. At last they sent for people to drag the pond. Then I could bear my dear mother's expression no longer, and, from my high window, I gave a little hoot. Instantly all was changed; Lea rushed upstairs to embrace me; there was great talking and excitement, and while it was going on, Uncle Julius was called away, and every one . . forgot that I had not been whipped! That, however, was the only time I ever escaped.'

Hare, *The Story of my Life*, 1896.

LADY HESTER STANHOPE
born March 1776.

I was always, as I am now, full of activity, from my infancy. At two years old, I made a little hat. You know there was a kind of straw hat with the crown taken out, and in its stead a piece of satin was put in, all puffed up. Well! I made myself a hat like that; and it was thought such a thing for a child of two years old to do, that my grandpapa had a little paper box made for it, and had it ticketed with the day of the month and my age.

＊

How well I recollect what I was made to suffer when I was young! And that's the reason why I have sworn eternal warfare against Swiss and French governesses. Nature forms us in a certain manner, both inwardly and outwardly, and it is vain to attempt to alter it. One governess at Chevening had our backs pinched in by boards, that were drawn tight with all the force the maid could use; and as for me, they would have squeezed me to the size of a puny

miss ... a thing impossible! My instep, by nature so high, that a little kitten could walk under the sole of my foot, they used to bend down in order to flatten it, although that is one of the things that shows my high breeding.

Memoirs of the Lady Hester Stanhope,
London, 1845.

ALEXANDER SOMERVILLE
born March 1811.

To return to the dear years of 1816 and 1817. I remember that on one occasion our potatoes had dwindled to very nearly none. Those left lay in a corner in the pantry behind the door, and my mother never went into the pantry without drawing a heavy sigh, and saying that she 'wondered what in the world would come of us when they would all be done.' Our door

opened into the straw close where a number of large, hungry, horned cattle were eating straw. They should have been eating turnips, but the turnip crop had been a failure that year as well as the potato crop. One of these animals had, unseen, made his way into the pantry, and was fast engaged in making a finish of our little stock of potatoes. I and my sisters Mary and Janet ... all children, and the only creatures near, except our mother, heard a noise in the pantry and ran to see what it was, and there was our poor mother battling with this horned ox to get him out, and to save the potatoes, he almost too large to turn, even if he had been willing to turn; but he was not willing. His hide and hair were so thick that he cared nothing for all the blows which our mother could give him. He kicked out with his hind feet, and kept eating. In desperation to save the potatoes, my mother got up to his head between his large horns and the wall, and backed him out with blows of the tongs, while he butted and tossed his head. It was a dreadful sight to us; when the brute was dislodged, our poor mother sat down and cried over the loss of the potatoes. We all cried too, and bitter tears they were which we shed, one and all of us.

Somerville, *The Autobiography of a Working Man*, 1848.

MICHELANGELO
born March 1475.

As an infant he was 'intrusted to the care of a woman who was the wife of a stone-mason, and who was also the daughter of a person of the same employment; hence Michel Angelo sometimes facetiously remarked, that it was no wonder he was delighted with a chisel, since it was given to him with his nurse's milk.'

Duppa, The Life of Michel Angelo
Buonarroti, 1806.

CHARLES NAPIER
born March 1786.

At the age of seven he was sent to the High School of Edinburgh. 'He succeeded on one occasion in obtaining the position of "Don," of head of the class to which he belonged, and so proud was he of this distinction, that to

commemorate the event, he ordered a sedan chair, the conveyance much used by ladies in those days, and was thus carried home in triumph to his father's house in George's Square.'
E. Napier, *The Life of Admiral Sir Charles Napier*, 1862.

DAVID LIVINGSTONE
born March 1813.

When he was ten years old he went to work in a factory as a piecer, and out of his first week's wages he bought Ruddiman's 'Rudiments of Latin.' Promoted to be a spinner after a number of years, he continued to devour all the books that came to hand except novels. His method was to place his

book on a part of the spinning-jenny so that he could catch sentence by sentence as he passed at his work.

Blaikie, *The Personal life of David Livingstone,* 1880.

WILLIAM COBBETT
born March 1762.

At eleven years of age my employment was clipping of box-edgings and weeding beds of flowers in the garden of the Bishop of Winchester at the castle of Farnham, my native town. I had always been fond of beautiful gardens, and a gardener who had just come from the king's gardens at Kew gave me such a description of them as made me instantly resolve to work in those gardens. The next morning, without saying a word to any one, off I set, with no clothes except those upon my back, and with thirteen halfpence in my pocket. I found that I must go to Richmond, and I accordingly went on from place to place inquiring my way thither. A long day (it was in June) brought me to Richmond in the afternoon. Two pennyworth of bread and cheese and a pennyworth of small beer which I had on the road, and one halfpenny that I had lost somehow or other, left threepence in my pocket. With this for my whole fortune, I was trudging through Richmond in my blue smock-frock, and my red garters tied under my knees, when, staring about me, my eye fell upon a little book in a bookseller's window, on the outside of which was written, 'The Tale of a Tub, price 3d.' The title was so odd that my curiosity was excited.

I had the threepence; but then I could not have any supper. In I went and got the little book, which I was so impatient to read, that I got over into a field at the upper corner of Kew Gardens, where there stood a haystack. On the shady side of this I sat down to read. The book was so different from anything that I had ever read before, it was something so new to my mind, that, though I could not understand some parts of it, it delighted me beyond description, and produced what I have always considered a sort of birth of intellect.

I read on until it was dark, without any thought of supper or bed. When I could see no longer, I put my little book in my pocket and tumbled down by the side of the stack, where I slept till the birds in the Kew Gardens awakened me in the morning, when off I started to Kew, reading my little book. The singularity of my dress, the simplicity of my manner, my lively and confident air, and doubtless his own compassion besides, induced the gardener, who was a Scotchman, I remember, to give me victuals, find me lodging, and set me to work; and it was during the period that I was at Kew that George IV and two of his brothers laughed at the oddness of my dress while I was sweeping the grass-plot round the foot of the Pagoda.

William Cobbett in a letter to the *Evening Post,* 1820.

GAMES
for the
MARCH
BABY

B O Peeper,
Nose dreeper,
Chin chopper,
White lopper,
Red rag,
And a little gap.

These lines are said to a very young child,
touching successively for each line the eye,
nose, chin, tooth, tongue, and mouth.
Popular Rhymes and Nursery Tales,
collected by Halliwell, 1849.

It is gratifying to learn that, notwithstanding
his injunctions regarding playthings of
primitive and simple antiquity, Scriblerus
condescended to allow his son Martin the use
of a few modern ones, such as might benefit
his mind by imparting early notions of

66

science. Even as nutcrackers taught him the use of the lever, swinging on the ends of a board the balance, bottlescrews the vice, whirligigs the axis and peritrochia, bird-cages the pulley, and tops centrifugal motion, he found the 'marbles taught him percussion and that laws of motion.' It will not be amiss here to add that bob-cherry was reckoned useful, since it taught 'at once two noble virtues, patience and constancy; the first in adhering to the pursuit of one end, the latter in bearing disappointment.'

Brand, *Antiquities*, 1888.

Move the forefinger very slowly round and round before the child, saying solemnly,

        'Heat an iron very hot,
        Stick a pig, very fat,
(Quickly)   Bore a hole, bore a hole, bore a hole!'
(Thrusting the outstretched finger at the child.)

Jackson, *Shropshire Folk-Lore*, 1883.

67

A
MARCH
CHILD
IN
FICTION

ME, I was very happy. Nobody paid any attention to me. I took advantage of this to play all day with Rusty in the deserted workshops, where our steps rang out as steps do in a church, and in the big deserted courtyards which the grass was already invading. This young Rusty, son of the keeper Colombe, was a big fellow for his dozen years of age, strong as an ox, devoted as a dog, silly as a goose and remarkable above all for the enormous shock of red hair to which he owed his nick-name, Rusty. Only, to tell the truth: Rusty, to me, was not Rusty. He was sometimes my faithful Friday, sometimes a crowd of attackers, sometimes a mutinous crew: anything I wanted. I myself during this time was not Daniel Eyssette. I was that singular man dressed in the skins of animals, the book of whose adventures had just been given to me, Mr Crusoe himself. It was an obsession. In the evening after supper I re-read my 'Robinson,' I learned it by heart. During the day I enacted it, I enacted it with intensity, and everything around me I made a part of my play. The factory was no longer the factory. It was my desert island . . . oh! How deserted it really was! The tanks served as the ocean. The garden was a virgin forest. There were in the plane-trees a lot of crickets who were in the play without knowing it.

Neither did Rusty imagine what an important rôle he played. If anyone had asked him who Robinson was, he would have been at a loss. Nevertheless I must admit that he put everything he had into his job, and that there was no one who could match him in imitating the roars of wild animals. Where had he learned how to do it? I cannot imagine. Anyway, those huge roars that he produced deep down in his throat while tossing his red mane would have made the bravest tremble. I myself, Robinson, sometimes felt unnerved by it, and had to whisper to him: 'Not so loud, Rusty. You scare me.'

Translated from Daudet, *Le Petit Chose*, 1877.

LETTERS
from
MARCH
CHILDREN

MARGARET MILLER DAVIDSON born 26th March, 1823. This letter of hers is dated 18th October, 1835.

'We are now at Ruremont, and a more delightful place I never saw. The house is large, pleasant, and commodious, and the old-fashioned style of everything around it transports the mind to days long gone by, and my imagination is constantly upon the rack to burden the past with scenes transacted on this very spot. In the rear of the mansion a lawn, spangled with beautiful flowers, and shaded by spreading trees, slopes gently down to the river side, where vessels of every description are constantly spreading their white sails to the wind. In front, a long shady avenue leads to the door, and a large extent of beautiful undulating ground is spread with fruit-trees of every description. In and about the house there are so many little nooks and by-places, that sometimes I fancy it has been the resort of smugglers; and who knows but I shall find their hidden treasures somewhere? Do come and see us, my dear uncle; but you

must come soon, if you would enjoy any of
the beauties of the place. The trees have
already doffed their robe of green, and
assumed the red and yellow of autumn, and
the paths are strewed with fallen leaves. But
there is loveliness even in the decay of nature.
But do, do come soon, or the branches will be
leafless, and the cold winds will prevent the
pleasant rambles we now enjoy. Dear mother
has twice accompanied me a short distance

about the grounds, and indeed I think her health has improved since we removed to New York, though she is still very feeble. Her mind is much relieved, having her little family gathered once more around her. You well know how great an effect her spirits have upon her health. Oh! if my dear mother is only in comfortable health, and you will come, I think I shall spend a delightful winter prosecuting my studies at home.'

A LETTER FROM ANOTHER MARCH CHILD

Charles De Rémusat was born on 14th March, 1797. On 18th November, 1806 his mother wrote to his father . . .

'When I was about to close my letter, Charles brought me one for you. This letter, which he wrote all by himself, is very clever, and I really regret not sending it to you, but I am afraid that it might get lost, and he naïvely gives you some family details that I do not in the least wish to get about. But, as I do not want to disappoint him by telling him that I have suppressed it, do, my dear, answer him as if you had received it …'

And this is the letter which Madame de Rémusat held back:

'Wednesday
I ask your pardon, my dear papa, for not having written to you sooner. Mama must have written to you about Gustave's accident, he is a little better, we are all well. I have been

to the museum, the pictures I like best are: "Jeanne de Navarre" and the pictures by Richard. I do not much like "Le Deluge." M. Halma is satisfied with me; I work more than at Auteuil. We go to my aunt's often; she is not very gay, because she is worried. It seems that the emperor is very successful, and that we are going into Berlin as we went into Vienna; his conquests are worse than those of Alexander or Cyrus. One can apply to Paris the line of Phèdre: *Humiles laborant ubi potentes dissident.* I am on Alexander and Demosthenes in M. Rollin now. I do not like Philip, because he is too ambitious. But I like you better than any of them. Good-bye, my dear papa; I send you my love.'

CHARLES.

Lettres de Madame de Rémusat, Paris, 1881.

RHYMES
for the
MARCH
BABY

MARCH brings breezes loud and shrill,
Stirs the dancing daffodil.
                    Sara Coleridge (1802–1852).

                                   Women know
The way to rear up children, (to be just),
They know a simple, merry, tender knack

Of tying sashes, fitting baby-shoes,
And stringing pretty words that make no
  sense,
And kissing full sense into empty words;
Which things are corals to cut life upon,
Although such trifles: children learn by
  such,

Love's holy earnest in a pretty play,
And get not over-early solemnised, . . .
But seeing, as in a rose-bush, Love's Divine,
Which burns and hurts not, . . . not a single
  bloom, . . .
Become aware and unafraid of Love.
Such good do mothers.
        Elizabeth Barrett Browning (1806–1861).

Rock-a-bye, baby,
The cradle is green;
Father's a nobleman,
Mother's a queen;
And Betty's a lady,
And wears a gold ring;
And Johnny's a drummer,
And drums for the king.

The Nursery Rhymes of England,
collected by Halliwell, 1843.

A PRAYER

Matthew, Mark, Luke, and John,
Bless the bed that I lie on!
And blessed guardian-angel, keep
Me safe from danger whilst I sleep!
The Nursery Rhymes of England,
collected by Halliwell, 1843.

GOODNIGHT
to the
MARCH
BABY

IF a genie could spring up beside your bed and offer you three wishes, what gifts would you choose for your baby? Would you like riches, beauty, and success, or would you choose qualities of character, courageousness both moral and physical, generosity, and persistence? It is fun to think and imagine, but would you, I wonder, choose anything? In all the fairy stories wishes are chancy things, apt to go wrong. In any case, would you really want to pick one gift more than another for your baby? Unlikely, almost certainly you will say, 'No thank you, Genie. Buzz off.' And then as you kiss your baby goodnight you will whisper, 'Little darling, I love you just the way you are.'

Noel Streatfeild